Grace,
words have power!
M.Wayne Ag ♡

To Mom,

Thank you for filling my life with books and teaching me that reading leads to success.

–Irina

Parts of Speech Parade

New York City

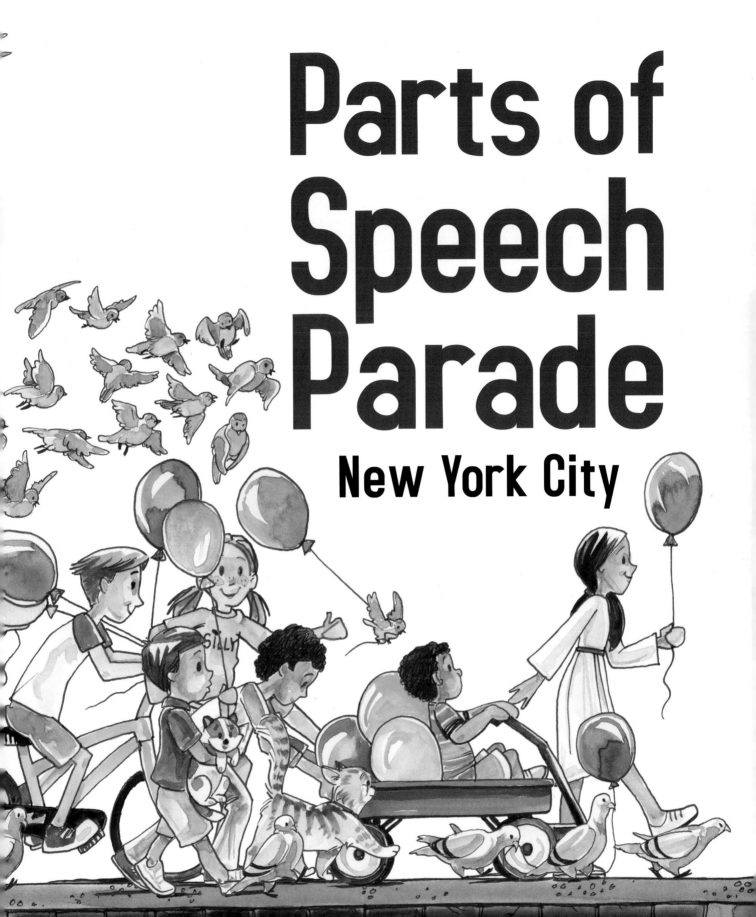

written by Irina Gonikberg Dolinskiy   illustrated by Mark Wayne Adams

Everybody say "Hooray!"
for the Parts of Speech Parade.

Let the Parts, while marching through,
introduce themselves to you!

I'm a person, place, or thing.
In a sentence, I am king.

"Who?" and "What?" shine in my crown.
Nice to meet you—I'm a NOUN.

I build, I work, I dance, I sing.
I'm an action, event, or state of being.

I help NOUNS act, and I'm superb.
The one, the only...I'm a VERB!

I am an ADJECTIVE, and I try to be true
when I describe the NOUNS to you.

Also, I identify NOUNS,
modify NOUNS, and quantify NOUNS.

Hello, I am a PREPOSITION.
And I am in the *best* position.

I put NOUNS in time and space.
So, thanks to me, each has its place.

When words need help to function,
they call me: the CONJUNCTION.

I connect words and subordinate,
correlate, and coordinate.

I'm an INTERJECTION! I express emotion.
I react to happiness, rejection, commotion.

Here are some phrases I can say:
"Ouch!", "Oh No!", "Wow!", and "Hey!"

Our Parts of Speech Parade is done.
Happy reading, everyone!

Now that you know our sound and look…

we'll see you in your favorite book!

Parts of Speech Parade

For more information regarding permissions,
contact Mark Wayne Adams, Inc., at:

Mark Wayne Adams, Inc.
PO Box 916392
Longwood, FL 32791
www.markwayneadams.com

Author: Irina Gonikberg Dolinskiy
Illustrator: Mark Wayne Adams
Editor: Jennifer Thomas
Designer: Mark Wayne Adams

First Edition, 2015

Summary: Children learn the parts of speech along their parade route.
Audience: Ages 3-8.
Library of Congress Control Number: 2014943698
ISBN-13: 978-1-59616-017-0
ISBN-10: 1-59616-017-9

Printed in Canada
Published in the United States of America

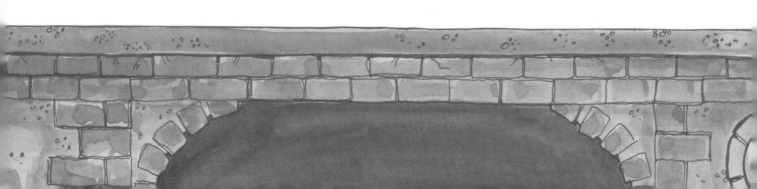